MAKING
BIG MONEY
DECISIONS

A Guide to Financially Navigating
Five Major Life Choices

EDWARD DOWNS

ISBN-13: 978-0-9995403-1-2

PUBLISHER: Edward F. Downs

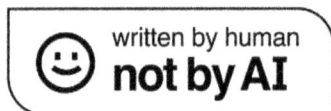

☺ written by human
not by AI

DEDICATIONS

To my children, Jackson and Mallory. Your Mom and I are immensely proud of the people you already are today, and excited for the people you will become tomorrow. We are here for you both if you ever need us for anything, but please keep <u>following your money</u>. We love you both so much!

ACKNOWLEDGEMENTS

To research and statistics professionals at public sector government and quasi-government agencies who are dedicated to collecting, maintaining, and sharing valuable finance and economics data. Your work made quantifying the concepts in my book possible. Thank you.

To my editors, Jordan Harris, Deborah Downs, and Jackson Downs. Thank you for taking the time to proofread and provide comments on my book. Your edits, insights and feedback made the final product better.

CONTENTS

INTRODUCTION

Did you know that the financial decisions you made or will make over your life can be worth millions of dollars in opportunity cost? **Opportunity cost** is the loss of potential gain from other alternatives when one alternative is chosen.

When that 'cost' is saved, it can generate substantial amounts of potential future financial value. I call this **"invested opportunity cost" or IOC.**

There are many financial decisions you will make in your life, but there are **five you may face in your lifetime** that can substantially impact the amount of money you accumulate for the future. These are:

1. Saving for retirement
2. Buying a car
3. Purchasing a house
4. Raising a child
5. Investing in a college education

After demonstrating how to calculate IOC for each of these major life choices, I share the story of **Jenna and Joe.**

Jenna and Joe used the concepts of IOC to make more- informed decisions and retire comfortably together at the ages of 57. Decisions that generated nearly **$6 million of IOC**, or the amount of financial value they created by making specific choices about how to spend and save their money over 31 years together.

Using IOC to make more-informed decisions was a **game-changer** for them, as it would be for most people in the pursuit of financial independence, early retirement, and a legacy of generosity.

Like Jenna and Joe, you too can generate substantial future financial value by making more-informed choices when making big money decisions.

In this book and on my website, you will find the **worksheets** to help you make more-informed financial decisions and potentially generate significant future wealth from IOC.

Reading this book is step one. Step two is applying these concepts to your life. If you want a head start on your calculations, then you can find the models in worksheets on my website at **DIYmoneytrack.com**.

PREAMBLE

Before we jump in, there are a few points worth highlighting.

Although the illustrations are based on sources from the United States of America, **the concepts are universal.**

This book is about financial planning and money management, not how to invest your money. Any references to specific investments are provided as examples.

I've created two characters, Jenna and Joe, to help you understand the financial concepts. They are fictional characters and any resemblance to real people is coincidental.

It's important that you understand the concepts and calculations driving the choices made by Jenna and Joe. For this reason, I have organized the book into two major parts.

- The first part provides you with the key concepts for making more-informed decisions and how to calculate IOC for each of the five major life events.
- The second part illustrates these concepts through the story of Jenna and Joe, and how they used IOC to navigate their big money decisions.

Think of the book as modular. You are welcome to skip ahead to second part to **Meet Jenna and Joe**, and circle back to part one afterwards as needed.

By making the **IOC worksheets** available on my website, my hope is that you apply these concepts to your own life and achieve financial freedom like Jenna and Joe.

The five life event chapters have been ordered in the book based on the timeframe most people are faced with these decisions. Your decisions may happen in a different order or at different times in your life, or not happen at all. For example, you may decide not to have any children, or raise children before purchasing a house.

There are situations you may face in life that are not covered in this guide, but the costs can influence the decisions you make in the five that are covered. Examples of these costs include:

- **Securing credit** – Building an excellent credit rating is foundational for getting the best rates on everything from mortgages to insurance. Information on best practices for building and managing your credit profile can be found at DIYmoneytrack.com.
- **Controlling debt** – Many young adults start their post-graduate lives in debt due to student loans. The cost of paying off student loans negatively impacts your ability to save for the future, and can result in taking on shorter-term debt, such as credit cards or auto loans, to fund lifestyle decisions. Using debt to acquire assets that appreciate in value such as education or housing, makes sense. Financing the purchase of assets that depreciate in value does not. Examples of depreciating assets include vehicles and other consumer goods. If you use a credit card or BNPL[1] to pay for these goods, then pay off statement balances every month or start using a debit card.
- **Managing risks** – Insurance provides you and your loved ones with a financial safety net if something bad happens. The cost of insurance needs to be factored into most of these

big money decisions. Useful articles on buying insurance can be found in the Resources section of DIYmoneytrack.com.

- **Owning a pet** can have emotional and health benefits, such as providing companionship, reducing stress, and increasing opportunities to exercise, get outside, and socialize. Like raising children, owning pets costs money with many "parents" underestimating the cost. According to Credit. com, "Based on the average life span of 12 years, the lifetime cost of owning a dog can range from **$20,000 to over $55,000**".[2] Although owning a pet generates quantifiable opportunity costs, I did not create a separate chapter since the typical expenditure amounts do not qualify it as a top 5 big money decision. Even so, I still recommend considering your IOC when making the decision to own pets.

- **Paying for healthcare** – Your cost of healthcare can have a major impact on your finances. Healthcare insurance and out-of-pocket costs need to be included in both current and future spending plans. According to Fidelity, an average retired couple may need approximately **$315,000** saved (after tax) to cover health care expenses in retirement.[3] And with healthcare inflation averaging about 3%[4] over last five years, that number will only continue to grow.

- **Caring for parents** – Providing financial support for your family, including parents, can stretch your finances and limit your ability to accumulate wealth. Families in this situation are often referred to as being part of the "sandwich generation." Any existing or forecasted expenses for parental care need to be factored into your plans. According to AARP, more than 78 percent of family caregivers incur some form of out-of-pocket expense. When it comes to total expenses, family caregivers spend an average of **$6,954** annually.[5] Don't let this cost be a surprise. Talk with your parents and in-laws about their current and future financial needs, so you can plan for your future.

KEY
CONCEPTS

Generating significant future financial wealth from IOC requires a plan and the discipline to keep it updated and carry it out.

For most of us, we can't control or count on earning our way to financial wealth, but the **decisions about how to spend money are more controllable**.

Emotions play a critical role in purchase decisions due mainly to great consumer marketing. Making a purchase decision based solely on the emotional aspects of a product or service, like its brand,[6] often leads to buying something you don't need, more than you need, or overpaying.

I created the concepts and worksheets to help you understand how to improve the rationalization of spending for big money purchases by adding the concept of IOC to your decision-making process.

Before we review the IOC for each of the five big money decisions, it's important to understand two foundational concepts that will help you succeed like Jenna and Joe.

The concepts are:

- Emotional versus rational decision-making and opportunity costs
- Your purchasing power and opportunity costs

EMOTIONAL VERSUS RATIONAL DECISION–MAKING AND OPPORTUNITY COSTS

Every time we purchase something we are using both emotional and rational decision making. However, while most people like to believe they are being rational in making decisions, it is usually the emotional side of the brain that is in the driver's seat, or as Baba Shiv, Professor of Marketing at Stanford Business School, puts it: "The rational brain is great at rationalizing what the emotional brain has already decided."[7]

This means that even the most pragmatic person is highly susceptible to emotional spending. We cannot help ourselves as deep down inside we are all creatures seeking emotional acceptance and comfort.

You are not alone. A LendingTree survey found that 69% of Americans say their emotions have influenced their spending and **76% of emotional spenders say doing so has led to overspending.**[8]

What motivates emotional spending is highly personal, whereas rational spending is often directed by more objective criteria. The major motives for rational and emotional spending can be found in Exhibit 1.

EXHIBIT 1

Rational	Emotional
Profit	Love/sentiment
Security	Pride
Utility	Envy
Caution	Entertainment
Health	Vanity

Source: Emotional vs Rational Purchases – How Social Media Triggers Consumers' Buying Decisions, ZABANGA Marketing (Oct 2023)

We make emotional decisions because we're human, not computers. Emotions can take over the buying process when you have been influenced into believing a product or service is more important than it really is.

We believe we 'need' something, when we really 'want' it. In some cases, you didn't really even 'want' it, but only bought it to fill an emotional need such as feeling stressed out, bored or unhappy.

When you feel regret after buying something you didn't need or overpaying, it's called **buyer's remorse**.

Buyer's remorse is surprisingly common among home buyers. According to a Zillow survey of buyers, 75% of those who had successfully purchased a home in the past two years had at least one regret about the home they bought.[9]

To achieve a feeling of status, comfort, or acceptance, like buying a big house or luxury car. Think about it: Why would a higher-income family of four 'need' to live in a house bigger than 3,000 square feet, or lease a $70,000 SUV? Usually, it's motivated by one or more of the emotions found in Exhibit 1.

We're under the influence. I'm not talking about "drinking and buying" but the intoxicating feeling you get from buying a product or service that is triggered by external sources. Product and service influencers can play a big part in what we buy, and are growing in importance thanks to the internet and social media.

Influencers can be people you don't know, like product marketers. They can also be people you know, like family, friends and neighbors. If you find yourself consciously thinking "what would [fill in the name] think or do" or admiring what others have, then you may need to seek some help.

Using recommendations or feedback to inform a purchase can be valuable, **if the ultimate decision also includes consideration for the impact to your finances.**

Businesses spend significant sums of money to emotionally connect you with their brands and products. Global advertising spending is expected to pass $1 trillion for the first time by 2024, according to WARC's Global Ad Spend Outlook 2023/24.[10]

Suffice it to say, professional marketers are paid to know you better than you know yourself, and understand exactly what emotional buttons to push to trigger your buying behaviors.

For big money purchases, like buying a house or purchasing a car, the combination of professional marketing and sales tactics can be a potent combination for overspending, if you are not prepared.

BIG AND SMALL MONEY DECISIONS

Emotional spending decisions impact all aspects of your personal finances, from small to big money purchases.

Smaller money spending decisions include making lower ticket purchases such as groceries, clothing, or electronics. When people don't budget or track spending, they often wind up buying more than they need, especially when it comes to acquiring smaller items.

Some of the reasons given by people for buying impulsively or over spending on smaller items are:

"I want to have the newest one"
"It didn't cost that much"
"I got a deal on it"
"I may need it at some point in the future"

Following your money for these spend categories ensures that you are staying within your budget and not overspending.

While you can more easily overcome poor purchase decisions for smaller money items, making a big money spending mistake can impact you in a way you may not have considered – your opportunity cost.

CONSIDER OPPORTUNITY COST WHEN RATIONALIZING BIG MONEY DECISIONS

As a refresher, opportunity cost refers to a benefit that a person could have received, but gave up, to take another course of action. An example of a big money opportunity cost is deciding to buy more house than you really need.

Overspending or paying for a house is usually driven by emotional decision making. By up-sizing the house, you are foregoing the opportunity to save and invest the money for the future (your IOC).

The opportunity cost is not only in the higher price you paid, but also in all the increased expenses, such as utilities and maintenance, which typically come with owning a larger home. And, if you financed the purchase with a bigger mortgage, then you'll be paying higher interest costs over the life of your loan.

Emotions play an important part in your decisions. Emotional spending is used in many cases to motivate your rational spending. As an example, your desire to provide a future for your children by investing in their college may be driven by love and pride.

Again, if those motives are backed up with spending choices that consider financial costs and benefits (including your IOC), then your spending decisions are more rational.

SO, HOW CAN YOU BE MORE RATIONAL IN YOUR DECISION-MAKING?

Here are steps you can take to make more rational spending decisions:

- Ask yourself what is the motive for making a purchase, and agree with your partner on the motive before buying.
- Follow a rationalization process with every purchase decision, big and small (see Exhibit 2).
- Consider the IOC of every purchase, but especially for big money decisions.
- Start *Following Your Money* to see the impact of spending decisions on your personal finances.

EXHIBIT 2

>>>>	(1) Identify Need/ Want	(2) Gather Information	(3) Evaluate Alternatives	(4) Make Purchase
Small Money	I need new shoes (rational motive= utility)	**How much can I afford to spend (budget allocation, financing)?**	What are the incentives (e.g., discounts available)? Where should I buy (shipping, returns)?	When should I buy? How should I pay for it?
Big Money	I/we want to buy a new house (rational motives= security, utility)	What are my product/ service preferences? What do reviewers say?	**What is the IOC of over spending or paying?**	Do I need to register my purchase (for updates, warranties)?

Source: DIYmoneytrack.com. For illustrative purposes.

PURCHASING POWER AND OPPORTUNITY COST

The second key concept is your purchasing power. Purchasing power refers to the number of goods or services that a certain amount of money can buy at a given time.

When consumer prices rise, your money can buy less. This is called "inflation"[11]. As prices drop, your money can buy more.

As reference, inflation had an average growth rate of about 1.9% per year over the past decade. However, at the time of this writing, the rate is closer to the average annual inflation rate of 3.7% for the past 50 years.[12]

If you're investing in college, tuition inflation is even higher, averaging 8% annually.[13]

As it relates to making big money decisions, understanding the changes in your purchasing power is important for planning purposes and calculating IOC.

If your income isn't growing faster than inflation, then you are losing purchasing power. For example, if inflation is growing at 4% per year and your income grows 3% in the same time, then you are losing purchasing power.[14]

Alternatively, if your income (after taxes) grows faster than inflation then you're increasing your purchasing power. As an illustration, if inflation grows 4% annually and your savings pay 6.5% or 4.9% annually after taxes[15], then you are increasing your purchasing power.

You can increase your purchasing power by:

- **Growing after-tax income from all sources faster than inflation**. Income sources may include wage (from annual merit, promotions), business, shorter-term savings and longer-term investments.
- **Reducing inflationary expenditures where possible**. Save more by minimizing spending on higher inflation goods and services. If you are interested in tracking price changes by consumer expenditure category, then visit the US Bureau of Labor Statistics website.[16]
- **Using rewards to lower spend amounts with cash-back credit card programs**. When applied to statement balances, these programs can reduce expenses by 2% or more[17] assuming you pay your balance in full each month and the merchant doesn't surcharge payments made with credit cards.

A gain in purchasing power means the same amount of money can buy more goods and services than before. This includes "buying" savings and investments.

When that "extra" money is saved in investments that compound over time, you have a catalyst for growing your wealth.

POWERING YOUR IOC CALCULATION

Understanding your purchasing power (rate of investment return less inflation rate) is important for calculating your IOC.

In calculating the IOC for scenarios in this book, I used an **estimated rate of return of 6.5%** for most of the illustrations. This amount, which represents an average of pre-tax value of savings from investment gains and inflation costs, can be changed in your calculations to reflect your risk tolerance and investment mix.

Living below your means (your income exceeds expenses over time) is the most controllable way to generate the savings necessary to fund your life goals.

If you are not actively managing your money by regularly tracking your spending and growing your purchasing power, then your ability to plan for big money decisions and generate IOC will be more difficult.

Please read my first book, *Following Your Money*, for a precise and practical DIY approach to tracking and managing your money.

Next, I'll introduce you to the five big money decisions and how to calculate the IOC for each one. After that, you'll meet Jenna and Joe and learn how they used these frameworks to make more-informed financial decisions, build considerable wealth, achieve financial independence, retire early and leave an inheritance.

BIG MONEY DECISIONS

1. Saving for retirement
2. Buying a car
3. Purchasing a house
4. Raising children
5. Investing in a college education

1

SAVING FOR RETIREMENT

"Retirement is a number, not an age."[18]

Concerningly, many Americans have not saved enough money for retirement.

For individuals aged 65 and above in the US, the average retirement savings balances are **$407,581**.[19] If you need to live off this money for 20 years, that works out to roughly $1,700 a month before taxes. If you add in the average social security payment of $1,667 per month,[20] that sums to approximately **$3,367** per month before taxes.

Is that enough? For the average person, it may not be enough. The average monthly expenditure for people aged 65 years or older is **over $4,000** per month, according to data from the most recent US Consumer Expenditure Survey.[21]

These data points tell me that the average American will need to decrease and control their expenses during retirement and/or find a way to increase their income **to keep from running out of money during their lifetime.**

Ideally, Americans nearing retirement should feel good about their situation, but most feel unprepared for retirement. According to the Board of Governors of the Federal Reserve System, although 84% of Americans aged 45 to 59 have retirement savings, **only 45% feel on track for retirement.**[22]

This is not surprising since **four in 10 Americans say they don't have a financial plan for retirement** and will just figure it out when they get there, according to an Allianz Life study.[23]

How do you feel about your retirement preparedness?

In this chapter, I'll provide guidance on how to estimate the amount of money you will need during your retirement, and the opportunity cost of not saving enough. We will also cover the surprising amount of value created by not overpaying for your investment fund returns.

FIGURING OUT YOUR RETIREMENT NUMBER

I was asked by a friend a few years ago if I've calculated the amount of money I need for retirement, and if so, how did I do it? I think he was surprised by my response that I first calculated the amount about 30 years ago when I started saving in a 401k retirement account and have been updating the plan numbers every year based on new information.

I asked him if he had a retirement plan and his response was that he's also been saving for retirement since he started working many years ago, but his "plan" was to save as much as he could, whenever possible.

This raises an important distinction: **Saving for retirement is not the same as planning for retirement.**

At some point you may have learned that if you save 10% of your earnings each year and retire at age 65 then you'll have a nice "nest egg" for retirement. While that may be enough, it may not be enough. A plan answers the questions:

- At what age do I want to, or can I, retire?
- How will I get there, considering other short and medium-term goals?
- What happens if my goals and plans change?

Answering these questions raises another important point: **Even having a plan is not enough**.

You must be prepared to update that plan based on more current events, such as unforeseen changes in income or expenses.

WHY PLAN FOR RETIREMENT?

There are many benefits associated with retirement planning, but the primary reason is to **make sure you have enough money to fund a comfortable lifestyle during retirement**. Secondarily, you may want to be able to leave money as inheritance for loved ones or to donate.

Moreover, if you are a parent or plan to raise children, then retirement planning **reduces the chance that you will be a financial burden on your children**.

I'm going to cover a couple of resources that will help you quickly determine how much you need depending on whether you are a long way from retirement or nearing it.

Keeping these numbers fresh is up to you.

I'M A LONG WAY FROM RETIREMENT (10+ YEARS AWAY)

Even if you're a long way from retirement it is important for you to perform some calculations to figure this out, since it is more than likely **the biggest investment you will make in your lifetime**.

Figuring it out early also allows you to compound money longer, a key catalyst for growing savings.

To build a more realistic plan, you will need to answer the questions above and estimate the 'cost' of achieving short, medium, and long-range goals; and then be prepared to adjust based on new information.

However, if you simply want to estimate how much you need as a starting point to your plan, I suggest using a retirement calculator, like the one available from Bankrate.com.[24]

As an illustration, a **25-year-old who has $75,000 in annual income** (growing equal to rate of inflation of 3.5%) and wants to **retire at 60 with $0 saved today** would need to **save 24% of their income**[25] on average per year to have enough saved to **live 35 years after retirement.**[26]

Alternatively, if that same person only saved 10% of their income, their retirement savings would **run out at age 72.**

The invested opportunity cost (IOC) of saving an additional 14% of income to cover 23 years of planned retirement funding is over **$2 million.**

An important consideration in using retirement calculators is whether to include Social Security.

If you are far away from retirement, then I recommend generating a plan with and without Social Security. Creating a plan without it will:

- Force you to boost your savings rate earlier in your life and benefit from longer compounding;
- Ensure that you have a safety net in case your plans change; and
- Give you options to decide on the best age to begin collecting your social security benefits.

Not to mention, Social Security policies such as the age you can start collecting full benefits or the amount you will get, may change by the time you are ready to retire.[27]

As you near retirement, you can more accurately build Social Security into your plan.

I'M NEARING RETIREMENT (5–10 YEARS OUT)

If you are nearing retirement, figuring this out is an imperative so that you can maintain or improve your lifestyle during your "golden years".

Start by projecting your expenses (including taxes) and income during your retirement years. To project these numbers, you need to know your current expenses and what changes will occur when you retire.

There are a few 'rules of thumb' you could use, but I recommend that you go through each expense category and estimate any impacts based on retirement plans. For example, are you planning to downsize your house or move to a state with a lower cost of living?

It's not only important to figure this out for financial purposes, but it will also spur you to **get on the same page with your partner**, as needed.

Another important consideration is when to take social security. To find out how much money you will get from social security visit the Social Security Administration website at www.ssa.gov and sign in/up to your account to see your current/projected benefits.

Now that you have a fair estimation of your expenses and income, plug it into a calculator[28] to see how long your money will last.

I use a worksheet that tracks and projects my family's finances. Using a spreadsheet allows me to estimate the future impact of saving and spending decisions over the next 20 years, and includes scenario planning and tactics for the conversion of investments into the cash needed to fund our lifestyle.

If you would like to find out more about this worksheet, please connect with me through DIYmoneytrack.com.

DON'T BE PASSIVE WHEN MANAGING INVESTED OPPORTUNITY COSTS

The S&P 500 Index measures the value of the stocks of the 500 largest corporations by market capitalization listed on the New York Stock Exchange or Nasdaq. The intention of Standard & Poor's is to have a price that provides a quick look at the stock market and economy.[29]

An S&P 500 Index Fund is an investment composed of stocks that are listed in the S&P 500 Index. Its performance will be nearly identical to the performance of the market index. Many exchange-traded funds (ETF) and mutual funds track the index.[30]

If you had invested $100 in the S&P 500 index 30 years ago (1993), you would now have about $1,848 – a total return on investment of 1,748%, or **9.98% per year**.[31]

In fact, the S&P 500 returns have been so consistent over time that most large cap equity funds haven't been able to beat this performance. Fewer than 10% of active U.S. stock funds managed to beat the benchmark over the last full 20-year period.[32]

In terms of what you pay for having professional investment firms manage your funds, it can **cost 4-5 times more** on average for an actively-managed fund versus a passively-managed one.[33]

Thus, if you had simply invested in a passively-managed S&P 500 index fund, then you would have done better than over 90% of professional stock investment managers and reduced your costs by 73% on average.

But that's not the end of the story.

Even if you had invested in a fund that tracks the S&P 500 index, you still could have under-performed depending on the fees you paid to the investment company that managed your money.

WHAT FEES DO I PAY?

There are several different fees you can pay for having investment companies manage your money, including commissions paid for trading, fund expenses, sales loads, redemption fees, or administrative fees in a 401(k) or other employer-provided retirement plans.

Although all of these fees are important and impact the net value of your holdings, I'm going to focus on the fund expenses.

Fund expenses, often represented as an expense ratio, are the cost for an investment company to operate a fund.[34]

Simply stated, this is the cost you pay for the fund to manage your money and is taken out of your return. As an example, if your annual return was 10% and the fund's expense ratio was 1%, your net return is 9%.

Even small differences in these fees can really add up, especially as your money grows.

HOW DO THESE FEES AFFECT MY MONEY?

As I mentioned previously, even if you invested in a passively-managed fund that tracks a major index like the S&P 500, the fees you pay will impact the amount of money you will get back from that fund. Here's an example that will really drive home the point.

Exhibit 3 includes two real investment funds that invest in the S&P 500.

EXHIBIT 3[35]

Comparing two S&P 500 index funds	Fund A (Actively managed)	Fund B (Passively managed)
Annual expense ratio	2.36%	0.03%
Annual cost	$239	$3
Total cost – 10 years	$2,496	$39
Future value after fees & expenses[36]	**$13,062**	**$16,240**
Loss in future value from fees & expenses	$-3,178	n/a
Average annual return – 10 years	8.49%	11.13%

Data source: FINRA Fund Analyzer

Even though these funds essentially have the same investment objective, the amount of money you would have made over the ten years you held these funds would be very different depending on which fund you owned.

If you had invested $10,000 in Fund A instead of Fund B, you would have **paid $2,457 more** in fees over ten years. Moreover, you would have **kept $3,178 more** in your returns if you had instead invested in Fund B – your opportunity cost.

That's a substantial amount of money for a $10,000 investment held for 10 years, but what if you invested in Fund A for your retirement?

Using <u>FINRA's Fund Analyzer,</u>[37] I compared these two funds using an initial contribution of **$500,000 held for 20 years.** Your IOC is the difference between the future value after fees & expenses of Fund A and Fund B, equal to over **<u>$400 thousand</u>**.

Interestingly, as consumers we may be cost conscious when making a large investment, like buying a house or paying for higher education, but most of us have no idea what we're paying to buy an investment fund or how much it will cost us down the road.

Maybe it's because the fees and costs are "hidden" in the returns, and therefore less transparent. Your investment portfolio may likely be the biggest asset you own in your lifetime, so how much it costs you should be a major factor in what you decide to buy.

2

BUYING
A CAR

If you are in the market for a new or used vehicle, then it is important to understand the potential future consequences of your choices. The main choices for buying a vehicle are:

1. What type of vehicle: make, model, year (new or used)?
2. How to fund purchase: pay cash, finance, or lease (rent)?

The answers to these questions will not only impact your current expenses, but will also have a major impact on your IOC.

WHAT TYPE OF VEHICLE?

Do some homework before you settle on the make and model. Here are a few things to consider before you buy that new or used vehicle:

- **A vehicle is a financial decision, not an emotional one.** Automobile companies and dealers do a great job marketing stuff that really doesn't matter for the majority of drivers, like style, luxury, and status. Unless you need your vehicle to impress clients for work, focus on the things that matter, like safety, reliability, and ownership cost.

- **Think of your vehicle as an asset that is used to create income or efficiently transport precious cargo, not a lifestyle**. The income is created by using your vehicle to commute to work, or do your work. The precious cargo is you and your loved ones. If you think of your vehicle as a 'use asset' then the most important financial criteria for selecting a vehicle is value, which can be found in the TCO, or **Total Cost to Own** amount. The TCO reflects all costs associated with owning and operating that vehicle over time and should be an important data point when deciding which one to buy.

You can obtain TCO and resale values for newer and older vehicles at Edmunds.com.

Another important consideration in deciding what type of vehicle to buy is the **resale value**. Resale value refers to what your vehicle will be worth when you try to sell it or trade it in the future.

A vehicle that loses its value faster than its rivals can cost you money in lower trade-in value or the possibility of owing more than it may be worth in a long-term loan.

If you are in the market for a new vehicle, Kelley Blue Book (kbb.com) provides annual information on new cars with best resale value.

For used vehicles, Consumer Reports (CR.org) provides a list of best used cars by price range.

HOW TO FUND THE PURCHASE?

In my book, *Following Your Money*, I presented an example of financing the purchase of a TV set by making the minimum monthly payment of your credit card. In this example, the total cost of the financed TV purchase was more than the resale value.

This same situation can happen whenever you finance a depreciating asset, such as a TV or a vehicle. Like other consumer products, a vehicle starts depreciating or losing value as soon as it is purchased.

Financing the purchase not only increases your current expenses, which negatively impacts your invested opportunity cost, but also reduces your resale value.

Exhibit 4 provides an example of how financing the purchase of a vehicle can reduce your resale value.

EXHIBIT 4

A	Purchase price of new car	$24,000	
After owning car for 5 years, you decide to sell it…			
B	Value depreciation	-$15,300	
With and without financing >>>>		**Loan**	**No Loan**
C	Interest paid on $24k loan (after 5 years)	-$4,116	$0
D	Your resale value of car (A+B+C)	$4,584	$8,700
E	Amount of loan balance, after sale	-$4,684	$0
F	Your resale value, after any loan repayments (D-E)	**-$100**	**$8,700**

Footnotes:
A. Includes all taxes and fees
B. Based on trade-in value of $8,700 on 2018 Chevrolet Malibu L 4D sedan with 60k miles and in very good condition, per KBB.com
C. Assumes 72-month auto loan from financing company at 5.5%. Total interest paid after 60-month is $4,116, based on amortization schedule (Bankrate.com Auto Loan Calculator)
E. Principal ($4,568) and interest ($116) payments remaining for the final year of loan.

In this case, the buyer financed the purchase of a new car with a 72-month auto loan from a finance company. After five years, the buyer wanted to sell the car for a different model.

The trade-in value of the car is $8,700[38], which means the car lost 64% of its value in five years.

After factoring in the **$4,116 the buyer paid in interest on the loan,** the real resale value is $4,584. However, since the buyer took out a 72-month loan due to lower interest rate, they still had to pay back $4,684 in principal and interest.

After paying off the loan, the buyer paid more than he/she received from selling the car a year earlier!

Had this buyer paid for the car in cash, then he/she would have $8,700 to use for purchasing another car. Hopefully, a used car with no loan this time.

WHAT ABOUT LEASING?

In this case, the buyer had considered leasing the car because of the lower monthly payments, but decided to finance the purchase at the time under the (faulty) assumption that they would own the car for longer than the loan period.

Leasing a new car over buying one typically results in lower and more predictable payments and ownership costs, but usually costs you more than an equivalent loan because you're paying for the car during the time when it is most rapidly depreciating.

"Over the long term, the cheapest way to drive is to buy a car and keep it until it's uneconomical to repair," according to Jon Linkov of Consumer Reports.[39]

Using a calculator like this one from Bankrate[40] can help you make a more informed decision about whether to lease or buy.

CALCULATING YOUR IOC FOR BUYING A CAR

The decisions you make on what vehicle to buy and how to pay for it impacts your IOC.

To calculate your IOC for buying a vehicle combine the savings from your monthly payments and difference in the TCO.

For example, by financing the purchase of a new car with a loan, the buyer in the prior case paid $392 per month. If the buyer decided to purchase a used car with savings (no loan), then he/she would have $392 per month to be used elsewhere.

Assuming that amount was instead saved for six years (the loan period), the total amount would be $28,224. Now, if you further assume that he/she invested that savings for 30 years,[41] the IOC would be about $**187 thousand**.

This represents the potential future amount he/she would have generated if they had not financed the car purchase.

Vehicles cost different amounts to own, calculated as TCO. If the buyer in the prior example purchased a car with a lower TCO, those "savings" could be invested. Exhibit 5 provides an example of how to calculate the IOC from the difference in TCO:

EXHIBIT 5

	Total Cost to Own[42]
Vehicle A – current car/choice	$36,236
Vehicle B – alternate choice	$31,000
Difference (A-B)	$5,236
IOC (30 years, 6.5% rate)	**$34,633**

By combining the IOC for both scenarios, the total potential IOC generated if the buyer had purchased the car for cash (no loan) and with a lower TCO is more than **$221 thousand**.

Think about what you can do with that amount of money in retirement. If so inclined, you could afford to buy a new RV (Recreational Vehicle) and travel across America for a few years.

3

PURCHASING A HOUSE

Even for the most fiscally disciplined people, emotions can creep into the buying decision for a house. People spend a lot of time in their houses, so aesthetics matter.

Combine that with savvy real estate agents and other influences, and there's a good chance you're going to overbuy or overpay to make a house your home.

When it's time to go house hunting, "the No. 1 thing you can do to set yourself up for success is leaving emotion out of the equation" say HGTV stars Drew and Jonathan Scott, better known as the Property Brothers.[43]

Often people will justify overbuying by considering their home as an investment or tax deduction, but the reality is a **house used as a primary residence is not a good investment historically <u>relative to alternatives</u>**.

For these reasons it is critical that you don't buy too much house.

RENT OR BUY?

The objective of this chapter is to provide you with a guide for making more-informed decisions when purchasing a home. Buying a house is a big money decision, but you may not be ready.

If you can't afford to buy right now or you don't plan to stay in the house for at least five to seven years,[44] then renting may be a better option.

Use an online rent-or-buy calculator, such as the one available from Zillow,[45] to figure out when it would be more advantageous for you to buy versus rent.

HOW CAN YOU ENSURE THAT YOU DON'T BUY TOO MUCH HOUSE?

If you are set on purchasing a house, then there are a few steps you can take to ensure that you don't buy more house than you really need:

- Calculate how much house you can afford;
- Think of your house as an investment, and prioritize savings instruments with higher growth rates; and
- Consider your IOC when deciding how much to spend on a house.

HOW MUCH HOUSE CAN I AFFORD?

If you are in the market to buy a house, then you should at a minimum figure out how much house you can afford.

Many people mistakenly believe they can 'afford' a house if they can cover the one-time down payment, closing costs, and the future monthly payments for a mortgage, taxes, and property/homeowners' insurance.

In looking at a typical homeowner's annual expenses, the cost for other housing-related expenses is **more than double** your mortgage interest and property tax expenditures based on the US Bureau Labor of Statistics most recent Consumer Expenditure Survey.[46]

- Monthly costs for mortgage interest and property taxes represent **6.8%** of the average US homeowner's annual expenditures.
- Other housing-related expenditures represent **14.8%** of household spending (Exhibit 6).

EXHIBIT 6

Expenditure category	Percent of avg after-tax income	% change from prior year
Utilities, fuels, and public services	5.5%	7.7%
Maintenance, repairs, insurance, and other expenses	3.1%	9.6%
Household furnishings and equipment	3.1%	-3.5%
Household operations	2.2%	12.9%
Housekeeping supplies	0.9%	-2.0%

Again, make sure to consider all associated costs when estimating how much you can most comfortably afford, and for calculating your IOC.

Using an affordability calculator from NerdWallet,[47] I calculated how much house the average US household with an average annual gross income of $94,000[48] could afford in northern NJ.

Assuming no current debt, a good credit rating and $30,000 available to make a down payment on a 7% 30-year loan, the average US household could afford a home worth about **$312,000**, with a total payment of around **$2,814 per month** for a mortgage, insurance, and taxes.

Remember, owning a home will result in other expenses, such as utilities, maintenance, and furnishings. Although most online calculators don't account for all of the added costs, you should estimate these budgetary increases and bake into your affordability estimate.

WHAT PERCENTAGE OF MY INVESTMENT PORTFOLIO SHOULD HOUSE EQUITY COMPRISE?

Your house is an asset, but your mortgage debt is a liability. The difference between the marketable price of your house and the principal amount of your mortgage loan is the equity value of your home.

So, if the market value of your home is $350,000 and your mortgage loan amount is $250,000, then your equity value would be $100,000.

That $100,000 in equity is an asset in your investment portfolio. Another type of equity asset in your portfolio may be company stocks (or stock funds).

Stocks and bonds (securities) have several advantages over house equity as an investment instrument, and over time should comprise a relatively larger portion of your investment portfolio.

The primary reason for prioritizing stock equity ownership is the return. Historically, stocks have offered better returns than real estate investments. Stocks have returned, on average, about 8% - 12% per year while real estate has generated returns of 2% - 4% per year.[49]

Other reasons why you want the equity value of your house to comprise a relatively smaller amount of your overall assets:

- It is easier to value and sell securities investments;
- Transaction costs for securities investments are much lower;
- Securities investments typically cost a lot less to hold/ maintain;
- You can't live off the value of your house in retirement if you're still living in it. Okay, technically you can with a reverse mortgage[50] but this is a costly borrowing option.

As a reminder, this only considers the change in value of investment from a primary residence. Investing in real estate as a landlord has the added benefit of growing regular income with tax advantages, but may require considerable maintenance costs.

CALCULATING THE IOC FOR PURCHASING A HOUSE

There are two ways to look at the financial impacts of buying a house at different price points. One way is cost savings, and the other is opportunity cost. The most effective way to show the impacts of cost savings and opportunity cost is with an illustration.

Assuming the buyer in the prior affordability example were considering two houses: House A costs $375,000, and House B $300,000.

If they decided to buy the more expensive House A, they would wind up paying **$104,612** more in mortgage interest assuming a 7% 30-year loan.[51] This doesn't include the added expenses for higher taxes, private mortgage insurance, homeowners' insurance, utilities, maintenance, and other household expenses.

Every dollar you put into buying a house has an opportunity cost. The opportunity cost could be investing in higher-growth savings or paying off more-costly debt.

Continuing with the example, assume the buyer bought the lower price home. By doing so, they would be saving **$549 per month** in mortgage interest, taxes, PMI, homeowners insurance and fees that would have been incurred with buying the higher priced house. If that $549 were invested each month, the value could grow to over $ 166,646 in 15-years and more than **<u>$607 thousand</u>** in 30-years.

To summarize, paying $75,000 more today to buy the more expensive house would not only cost over $500 a month in added expenses, but also cost a buyer the missed opportunity to generate over $600k by investing those 'savings' over the next 30 years.

That amount of money could make a big difference in their retirement plans.

4

RAISING A
CHILD

Raising my beloved children with my wife will be my greatest accomplishment in life.

Raising a child is emotionally gratifying but rarely financially rewarding. Children are an expensive proposition that many young adults are not adequately prepared for financially.

Even parents in good financial condition often underestimate the cost of raising another child, especially when you add in the cost of paying for higher education.

THE COST TO RAISE A CHILD

According to the Brookings Institution, the average middle-income family with two children will spend **$310,605** to raise a child up to age 17.[52]

However, most parents' financial responsibilities do not end when their child turns 18 years of age. Also, the Brookings' statistic represents a national average and costs can vary depending on where you raise the child.

Using the Family Budget Calculator from the Economic Policy Institute,[53] you can more accurately find the basic costs based on where you live.

Basic costs include rent, food, transportation, child care, health care, taxes, and other items of necessity. It does not include savings/costs for higher education.

USING THE FAMILY BUDGET CALCULATOR

The calculator allows you to estimate the costs for families of different sizes, up to four children. With this data, you can extrapolate the incremental costs associated with adding children.

As an illustration, I used the Family Budget Calculator to find the incremental costs for a family of two adults with up to four children raised in Bergen County NJ.

The average annual incremental cost of adding from one to four children to a family is included in Exhibit 7.

EXHIBIT 7

Two adults living in Bergen Country NJ (in US dollars)

# of children	Monthly costs	Annual-ized costs	Incremental Annual Costs	Total Incremental Cost Over 18 years
None	5,424	65,088	n/a	n/a
One	7,590	91,080	25,992	581,866
Two	9,219	110,628	19,548	437,608
Three	11,017	132,204	21,576	483,008
Four	11,694	140,328	8,124	181,867

For example, the added budgetary cost for raising a first child would be $25,992 per year on average for a couple living in Bergen County NJ.

Adding a second child would cost you $19,548 annually on average, a third $21,576, and a fourth $8,124. Please visit the Economic Policy Institute's website[54] if you are interested in learning how these statistics were generated.

Another way to evaluate the cost of having additional children is by considering the IOC.

CALCULATING THE IOC FOR RAISING A CHILD

As an example, if a family living in Bergen County NJ decided to raise three children instead of two, then they would incur an additional $21,576 per year in expenses to raise the third child, per the Family Budget Calculator.

Assuming they did not incur those added expenses, they could have invested those annual cost "savings". If those savings were invested annually over 18 years, the IOC would be nearly **$700 thousand**.

The number is even larger if you include savings associated with paying for higher education costs.

The average cost for investing in a public college education in the US is $26,027 per year or **$104,108** over four years according to the Education Data Initiative.[55] For a private college education, the average cost to obtain a four-year degree is **$223,360**.

If you factor in lost income and loan interest, the ultimate price of a bachelor's degree may be as high as **$509,434** per the Education Data Initiative.

The IOC for investing the "cost savings" over 30-years using this data[56] is:

- **<u>$689 thousand</u>** for a public in-state college
- **<u>$1.5 million</u>** for private college

Under either scenario, your IOC for raising a child in Bergen County NJ and paying the full cost of a four-year degree is **well over $1 million**, and closer to $2 million if you invest in a private education.

Considering the financial implications, choosing how many children to raise may likely be the most important financial decision you and your partner make together.

Remember, raising a child that you cannot afford not only impacts your future but theirs as well.

5

INVESTING IN A COLLEGE EDUCATION

Getting the greatest value or highest return on your invested money should be a goal for every dollar you spend in life.

As the dollar value of that investment goes up so does the importance of making a more-informed decision. Like buying a house, investing in college for yourself or a child is one of those big money decisions.

While the decision about which school is the "best fit" is somewhat subjective, the cost benefit of obtaining a diploma can be viewed more objectively.

To help you evaluate that decision, you should consider it rationally by answering the following questions when investing in a college education:

1. Is it worth it?
2. How much does it cost?
3. What is the IOC of my different choices?

IS A COLLEGE DEGREE WORTH THE INVESTMENT?

Research from Georgetown University shows that the higher the level of educational attainment, the larger the payoff.

Bachelor's degree holders generally earn **75% more** than those with just a high school diploma, according to "The College Payoff," a report from the Georgetown University Center on Education and the Workforce.[57]

The report found that individuals who finished college earn a median of **$1.2 million more** than high school graduates over their lifetimes.

HOW MUCH DOES IT COST?

As referenced in the prior chapter, the average cost depends on your degree type and the institution you attend. For example, the annual cost of obtaining a 2-year Associate's Degree at a local community college is approximately one-eighth (i.e., 87% less expensive) the cost of a 4-year Bachelor's Degree at an in-state University.

Assuming you've made the decision to obtain a 4-year bachelor's degree, your costs will vary depending on the type of institution you attend.

Per the Education Data Initiative statistics, the average **Cost of Attendance (COA)**[58] by institution type can be found in Exhibit 8.

EXHIBIT 8

Institution Type	Avg Annual COA	Avg 4-Year COA
4-year public college, in-state	$26,027	$104,108
4-year public college, out-of-state	$27,091	$108,364
4-year private college	$55,840	$223,360

Please note that these costs represent the "sticker price" and do not include any incentives offered by the school, such as scholarships and grants. Also, these costs are based on data from 2021. If you are planning to invest for future attendance, you will need to inflate the costs.

To estimate the total cost over 4 years, you should plan at a minimum to increase costs each year as a starting point. For actual budgeting purposes, update with price changes from the schools.

Using the data above, if I increased the annual COA by 4.8% per year[59] over four years, then the totals increase by:

- **$7,739** to $111,847 for 4-year public in-state college
- **$16,603** to $239,963 for a 4-year private college

DOE COLLEGE SCORECARD

Another great resource for finding and comparing information about specific higher education institutions is the U.S. Department of Education (DOE) College Scorecard portal at www.collegescorecard.ed.gov.

The College Scorecard allows you to search and compare schools, as well as specific fields of study. In addition to key statistics on acceptance and graduation rates and median earnings, you can find costs by family income levels and financial aid & debt data.

Unlike the data in Exhibit 8, the cost represents the average "net price paid" and includes tuition, living costs, books and supplies, and fees minus the average grants and scholarships for federal financial aid recipients.

CONSIDERING YOUR INVESTMENT RETURN WHEN EVALUATING COLLEGES

To aid prospective students and their parents in more easily comparing and prioritizing the relative financial value of different colleges, I created the College Effectiveness Score (CES).

CES is a single number that measures a college's ability to effectively transition its students to a profession/career. Specifically, CES is a benefit-cost analysis that compares the annual earnings of students after graduating college to the net price paid for going to that college.

If you are interested in learning more about CES, please visit DIYmoneytrack.com.

CALCULATING IOC FOR INSTITUTION TYPE

Public, state-run colleges not only offer excellent educations but many rank highly when considering return on your investment.

Based on the most recent analysis, **8 of the top 10 CES scores were public state-run colleges** offering bachelor degrees.[60]

The decision to pay more for a private college education has an opportunity cost.

Based on Exhibit 8 data, the difference between a private college and public in-state college over 4-years is **$119,252**.

If you invested the $119,252 saved over 4-years from attending a public in-state college, your IOC would be more than **$420 thousand**.

Now that you understand how IOC can be used to inform your big money decisions, read on to learn how Jenna and Joe applied these frameworks to make more-informed financial decisions, build considerable wealth, achieve financial independence, and retire early.

MEET JENNA AND JOE

Jenna & Joe, both 57 years of age, recently retired from working for someone else. The couple have been married for 29 years and together for a total of 31 years. Together, they have been planning for this milestone for about 28 years.

The next chapter of their lives includes spending time with friends and family, volunteering, exercising, traveling, downsizing their estate, and enjoying other leisure activities such as golfing and pickleball.

HOW DID THEY GET HERE?

In looking back on their life, Jenna and Joe estimate that the calculated decisions made together over nearly 30 years have amounted to **$5.9 million in invested opportunity cost (IOC)** generated and saved in their financial accounts.

An amount that they estimate has contributed about **70%** of the value to their investment assets with a total value of **$8.5 million** at age 57. The other 30% coming from real estate investments, equity compensation Jenna received from one of her employers, and inheritance.

With the same values and fiscal discipline, Jenna and Joe were able to get consensus on how to execute by openly discussing plans and proposals with each other. Importantly, they also shared their plans with their parents and children.

A common bond was their shared belief in planning and saving for the future after college, and started following their money. First separately, and then together.

The key to their relationship and financial success:

- Setting goals together
- Celebrating milestones
- Always being transparent and honest

Jenna and Joe also benefited from preparing their children well. As role models and DIY finance aficionados themselves, Jenna and Joe did not rely on the school system to teach their children about personal finance.

After saving money from summer jobs and graduating college without loans (thanks to Mom and Dad), their children **began their adulthood in good financial shape**. When they both started jobs with benefits, Jenna and Joe stopped paying for most of their living expenses.

PLAN ORIGIN

About a year after being married and three years after they started dating, Jenna and Joe started developing their joint plan after reading *Making Big Money Decisions*.

Before working out the math, they started by aligning on answers to important life questions:

- *When they wanted to have children?* While dating, they had discussed "wanting" two or three children.
- *Where and when they wanted to purchase a house?* Assuming a house in the suburbs with reasonable commute to jobs and at least three bedrooms.

- *What type of family car would they need and when?* Both currently had cars, but Joe would trade-in his car for a family vehicle.
- *How much would they need to save to retire by age 55, and pay for both of their children's college?* A lot.
- *What was the physical and financial condition of their parents?* Fortunately for Jenna and Joe, both sets of parents were in good financial condition. Physically, Joe's father had recently been diagnosed with cancer at age 60, but it was caught early and the longer-term prognosis was good.

At the time, Jenna had a corporate job, earning $115k annually and Joe was a non-union contractor making $70k per year, for a total combined pre-tax wage income of **$185k**.

They rented an apartment together and lived well below their means, saving 70% of their "Fun Money"[61] discretionary income each month.

In addition to saving a large portion of after-tax Fun Money to joint savings and brokerage accounts, both were regularly saving 10% of their pre-tax wages to their individual 401k accounts. Each worked for companies that generously matched a percentage of their retirement contributions.

Looking back, Jenna and Joe both read *Following Your Money* right after finishing college. By tracking spending and aggressively prioritizing savings for over a decade after college, they were able to impressively accumulate a combined brokerage and retirement investment portfolio of **$700 thousand**. A good portion of it comes from the retirement matching contributions offered by their respective employers and automatic reinvestment (compounding).

This didn't include the $90 thousand they received as inheritance from Joe's grandmother, which they would use for the downpayment on their first house.

HAVE YOU MET JENNA

If you read *Following Your Money*, you met Jenna. Jenna had just graduated college and was one year into her new job. She was considering how to fund graduate school while continuing to increase savings when she started using a few worksheets for following her money.

Jenna's understanding and appreciation for managing her personal finances was a game-changer. She now had the tools and capabilities to determine how to fund her life goals.

Jenna also benefited emotionally from controlling her finances. She felt more satisfied with life and was more confident about her future, which improved her relationships with friends, family, and coworkers.

Like many young adults, Jenna was first introduced to basic financial literacy concepts in High School, but didn't get serious about managing her money until after college when she started collecting a salary and paying for all living expenses including student loans. *Following Your Money* gave her concepts and tools to track her money and financial condition.[62]

After moving back with her parents for a few years, Jenna moved to a smaller city near the larger city where she worked. Rent was more affordable and she could keep her car. Jenna prioritized saving by putting the maximum contributions in her 401k, taking advantage of her employer's generous contribution matching program.

She also generated savings by living below her means, adding those savings to her savings and brokerage accounts to build her "Glad Money" emergency fund.

Jenna decided to attend graduate school, but chose to go part-time while working and take advantage of the training, education & development benefits offered by her employer.

Although it took her a year longer to complete her master's degree requirements going part-time, she graduated with no additional debt. Her company paid most of the tuition and Jenna paid for rest from gifts and savings.

JENNA MEETS JOE

Jenna met Joe through a mutual friend and began dating at age 26. They connected by sharing complementary qualities but the same values, forming a strong life partnership. Joe lived in a nearby town and worked for an electrical and telecommunications contractor as an electrician.

As DINKs ("Dual Income No Kids") with relatively low necessary living expenses, they generated a lot of Fun Money. They saved most of their Fun Money each month, but used some of the savings to take a trip to Europe, and move in together before marrying.

Their wedding was small, with the cost fortuitously covered by Jenna's parents. Joe's parents paid for their honeymoon trip to the Bahamas.

After marrying, they agreed to merge their assets and liabilities by consolidating accounts to follow their money and make financial decisions more easily.

Both Jenna and Joe were in great financial condition prior to agreeing to merge their assets.

With an aggressive saving and investing plan, Jenna's retirement savings grew from $3 thousand after her first year of work to $450 thousand at age 30. Joe also saved proficiently starting in high school with total savings of $250 thousand.

Jenna and Joe had combined investment savings worth **$850 thousand**,[63] and were well on their way to joining the "millionaires club." But they were not clear on how much would be needed to live comfortably for more years than they worked, fund big money goals like raising children, and leave a legacy behind.

With a combined wages of over $185 thousand/year, short-term savings of $150 thousand, long-term savings in retirement accounts of $700 thousand and zero debt they were doing well, but had lots of life goals and both wanted to retire from working for paychecks in their 50's.

Additionally, Jenna and Joe both received annual bonuses from work. They allocated that money to their "Glad Money" emergency savings and a vacation fund budget.

Jenna agreed to manage their consolidated finances going forward and share updates with Joe each month.

BIG MONEY DECISIONS MADE

Fast forward 28 years.

Jenna and Joe have not only achieved their goal of retiring in their 50's, but raised two confident and ambitious children.

Using IOC to inform their big money decisions was a major factor in achieving financial independence and retiring comfortably by the age of 57.

For the five major life milestones, they estimate that IOC decisions generated nearly **$6 million** toward their current wealth.

Here's a summary of how they did it.

SAVING FOR RETIREMENT

Initially Jenna used a calculator[64] to estimate the amount they would need to retire at 55 and live at 80% of future expenses, while also leaving an inheritance.

If they wanted to live from savings for 40 years and leave a financial legacy, then they would need to save nearly 40% of their income and amass retirement savings of over $9 million.

To achieve this audacious goal, they knew that they would need to make optimal spending decisions and aggressively ramp up savings.

They increased the amount of income they put in retirement savings accounts **from 10% to 25%**. The incremental value of making this change generated nearly **$2.6 million** over 30 years of investing.

As they got closer to retirement, Jenna realized that they could fund their retirement lifestyle with lower expenses then initially planned. By making a smaller vacation home their primary residence and removing other expenses, they would be able to lower their annual expenses during retirement by **33%**.

BUYING A CAR

Joe was really into European vehicles, having owned multiple cars manufactured there for years. The cars were fun to drive, but maintenance and repairs were expensive.

When the time came to agree on a family car, Joe really wanted to buy a new luxury SUV from a European manufacturer, a beautifully designed and engineered vehicle. They had just received inheritance from Joe's grandmother and he felt they were able to 'treat' themselves.

Jenna felt that money should be used for buying a house. To change Joe's mind, she needed to prove to him that it made more sense to purchase a used car for cash.

Using the worksheet found on DIYmoneytrack.com, Jenna ran the numbers and estimated that they could generate a future financial value of **$410 thousand** in IOC from buying a used car with lower TCO. You can find her worksheet on my website.

Joe was convinced, and agreed they should use savings to purchase a three-row SUV with lowest mileage. He also agreed that his car should be used as a trade-in for their "new" car to lower the purchase price.

They wound up driving the family car for 14 years and 182,000 miles before encountering a major repair, and deciding to buy another newer used vehicle.

PURCHASING A HOUSE

Jenna and Joe bought their first home at ages 31, after viewing 10 different properties.

Before shopping around, they narrowed prospective towns by location (work commuting distances, access to mass transportation, proximity to family, home affordability) and quality of the school systems.

The first thing they did was estimate how much house they could afford. With $90 thousand to use as a downpayment, zero debt and excellent credit, they used a couple of different calculators to determine that they could afford a home worth between $600 - $700 thousand in their target town of Fair Lawn NJ.

When house hunting, they decided to look at houses priced between $425 thousand and $700 thousand, with the low-end representing an amount where their downpayment of $90 thousand would cover 20% or more of the price.

Putting 20% or more down on their home meant a lower mortgage interest rate and smaller monthly payments. It also meant they would not have to pay PMI, or private mortgage insurance.[65]

They found two houses that met all their criteria, both in good condition but at different price points.

At the higher end was a three-bedroom with more square footage that was recently renovated costing $650 thousand.

At the lower-end was a three-bedroom house priced at $450 thousand with a smaller property that could use some updating in future.

Next, they considered the IOC of buying each property.

Although they could afford to buy the higher priced property, they estimated that purchasing the lower priced property would **save them $1,780 per** month in mortgage principal and interest, property taxes, home insurance, and utilities.

Investing that amount for 15-years (the time they lived in the house) generated an IOC of **$540 thousand**.

They used some of their savings to update the kitchen and landscaping, and re-paint the entire house. After living in the house for 15-years, they sold it for a big profit and used the increased equity to make a large down payment on a new house and buy their first investment property.

RAISING CHILDREN

When dating, Jenna and Joe discussed how many children they wanted and how to raise them religiously.

Joe came from a family with four children and Jenna from three. They agreed on a plan to start by having two children and go from there.

After the difficult birth of their second child, they started reconsidering the idea of having a third child.

While the experience of childbirth for Jenna and Joe heavily influenced their decision, they also considered the financial implications of raising a third child.

Using data from the Family Budget Calculator, the incremental annual cost for raising a third child to age 18 in their home county was $21,576 per year. The IOC of this decision was nearly **$700 thousand**. Add in the cost of paying for college and the total investment for raising a third child could cost over $500k, with a potential IOC over **$1.3 million**.

Considering these financial implications made their decision easier.

INVESTING IN COLLEGE EDUCATIONS

Like many families, Jenna's parents could not afford to pay the full cost for her to attend college, so she needed to obtain a student loan.

She applied to colleges in her family's state of residence, as well as a few out-of-state public and private universities in hopes of securing academic scholarships to lower tuition costs.

She was accepted at a private college but did not receive enough money from the institutions to justify the expense.

This was a very difficult decision for Jenna since she felt a strong connection to one of the schools, and a good friend from high school was planning to attend. She even called the school to see if they could offer additional support, but they were unable to increase her financial aid package.

Jenna enjoyed her four years at state college and graduated with multiple job offers in her field. Her parents and grandparents pitched in for room & board for the two years she lived on campus, but Jenna graduated with student loans.

Jenna set a goal with Joe to save enough to pay for their children's college education.

After retirement savings, Jenna and Joe made saving for their children's education their next highest priority. They started automatically saving monthly income to 529 plans[66] and their brokerage account immediately after each child's birth. They also saved gifts from Joe's parents for their "Kid's education fund."

They saved aggressively and sold equity awards to fund state college educations for both of their children. Their first child wanted to attend the same in-state college where her mom graduated because it was well-regarded in her specific field of study.

The cost difference between deciding to attend their in-state college over a private university is estimated by the Education Data Initiative (educationdata.org) to be $119,252 over four years.

When that difference was instead invested, it grew to over **$420 thousand** in value over 20 years. Jenna and Joe planned to set aside some of these savings to help pay for their grandchildren's education.

ADDING IT UP

When Jenna and Joe added it all up, they came up with nearly **$5.9 million** in IOC from making more-informed big money decisions.

	Decisions made by Jenna and Joe	IOC Value
1	Saved 25% of income vs. 10%	$2,557,483
	.. and invested in lower cost index funds	$544,162
2	Bought a used car with no loan and lower TCO	$410,481
3	Purchased a less expensive house	$540,310
4	Not raising a third child	$699,280
	.. and not paying for third child to attend college	$688,608
5	Sent a child to in-state public college instead of private college	$420,202
	Total IOC	**$5,860,526**

Definitions:

- *Opportunity Cost* = The loss of potential gain from other alternatives when one alternative is chosen.
- *Invested Opportunity Cost (IOC)* = The value that would be created by investing the opportunity cost for the purpose of creating future wealth.

NOW IT'S YOUR TURN

Even if you don't have the same level of income or savings as Jenna and Joe, you will benefit from using IOC to make more informed financial decisions.

At a minimum, plan out your life to ensure you can enhance your post-work lifestyle. Assume you live to 90, 95, 100. *How much do you need?*

If you're up to the challenge, calculate your own IOC when making big money decisions and see if it amounts to millions in financial value like it did for Jenna and Joe.

What makes this all possible?

- **Generating steady and growing income.** Jenna and Joe both had stable jobs that paid them well, and offered other forms of incentive income like raises, bonuses, promotions, and equity. They also took full advantage of healthcare and retirement benefits offered by their employers. They were able to turn their income sources into nearly $6M in financial wealth from IOC. Use your income sources to chart your path to financial independence.

- **Saving relentlessly.** Both Jenna and Joe were taught the importance of saving at an early age by their parents. After Jenna took financial literacy class as a senior in high school she was hooked. Joe, always a diligent saver of his money, was motivated to move out of his home when he turned 23, a year after obtaining his electrical contractor license. They saved an impressive amount of money during their 20's and seriously ramped it up at age 30, giving them nearly **40 years** to compound their savings.

- **Controlling your expenses now and in the future**. Make rational decisions to minimize expenses so you can save more when younger, and downsize expense-generating assets so you can live longer from those savings when you're older. When their income increased over time, Jenna and Joe did not increase spending at the same rate, which boosted their purchasing power.
- **Opening an in-house bank**. When you save money in non-retirement accounts, you can use those deposits to loan yourself money. The money should be paid back from income over time, but at least you won't have to worry about interest rates or other bank fees. I'm not in favor of lending money to your children, since it is important for them to build a credit history and learn how to live within their means. Instead, allocate some of your savings to a "Kid's Gift Fund," but only give the money to them when they invest in (potentially) appreciating assets, such as paying for higher education, buying a house, or getting married.
- **Using digital applications to make money management easier**. DIY money management is a necessary skill for most people. Start following your money as soon as you start getting it, no matter how small. Learn how to use a spreadsheet application like Microsoft Excel or Google Sheets. Use worksheets or other digital applications to track your indicators of financial condition and map out the future. Allocate all money from your financial accounts to fund life goals. Optimize cash balances in line with spending needs through use of short-term investments such as High Yield Savings, Bank-issued CD's, Treasuries, Corporate's, and Muni's.

If you would like to use the worksheets from my books, just go to the Resources section of <u>DIYmoneytrack.com</u>.

I'm "open-source". You are welcome to download any worksheet from my website and customize it. I know people who use apps like Quicken and YNAB to manage their money that also use worksheets to analyze data, build models, and predict their financial future.

You decide which tools to add to your money management toolbox, but don't let them collect dust.

Start building for your future today!

THE BUILDING BLOCKS SUMMARIZED

SAVING FOR RETIREMENT

The IOC from contrasting savings rates and investment fund expenses.

Why is it important? Live more comfortably during your retirement and leave a financial legacy to make other people's lives better.

Concepts/frameworks:
- Compounding
- Matching
- Purchasing power
- Cost of investing (Fund expense ratio)
- Spending/expense control and planning

Tools:
- Retirement Plan Calculator
- Compound Interest Calculator
- Social Security Administration
- How Long Will Your Savings Last Calculator
- FINRA Fund Analyzer

BUYING A CAR

The IOC from contrasting car buying and ownership costs.

Why is it important? Car ownership means minimizing maintenance costs, maintaining resale value, and reducing opportunity cost.

Concepts/frameworks:
- New or used vehicle
- Cash, loan, lease pros and cons
- Resale value
- Total Cost to Own (TCO)

Tools:
- Car affordability calculator
- Kelley Blue Book
- Edmunds True Cost to Own
- Used car prices and best values
- Compound interest calculator (for IOC)

PURCHASING A HOUSE

The IOC from contrasting property ownership and related housing decisions and associated costs.

Why is it important? House ownership means minimizing maintenance costs, maintaining resale value, and reducing opportunity cost.

Concepts/frameworks:
- Building an excellent credit rating
- How much house can I afford?
- All in costs
- What is my house worth?

Tools:
- Credit score and monitoring services

- Affordability calculator
- Mortgage loan calculator
- Compound interest calculator (for IOC)
- Market value of your home, e.g., Zillow Zestimate

RAISING A CHILD

The IOC from contrasting opportunity costs for incrementally raising children to adult age and paying for college.

Why is it important? Next to saving for retirement, this could be your biggest expense and opportunity cost. For many, this one may be viewed as less "controllable" than saving for retirement, but figuring out how many children you can afford to raise is a big money decision.

Concepts/frameworks:
- Family Budget Calculator from Economic Policy Institute

Tools:
- Family Budget Calculator
- College calculators below
- Compound interest calculator (for IOC)

INVESTING IN A COLLEGE EDUCATION

The IOC from contrasting opportunity costs for a student to attend public state and private colleges in the US.

Why is it important? Affording to pay for some or all your child's education is rewarding for you and them, but it should not be done at the expense of saving for your retirement.

Concepts/frameworks:
- Is college worth it?
- Is going to graduate school worth it?
- ROI for colleges and fields of study

Tools:
- College cost and savings calculators
- College Effectiveness Score (CES)
- College Scorecard from US DOE
- Graduate school ROI calculator
- Return on Diploma (ROD) worksheet
- Compound interest calculator (for IOC)

NOTES

Thank you for Reading My Book!

THANK YOU

I need your feedback to make the next version of this book and my future books better.

Please leave me a helpful review on Amazon letting me know what you thought of the book.

Thanks so much!!

~ Ed Downs

ABOUT THE AUTHOR

Ed is a financial solutions expert, with over 30 years' experience developing and delivering innovative products and capabilities that empower individuals and organizations to outperform, while contributing to the success of the Federal Reserve Bank of NY, Citigroup, and Mastercard. He is passionate about helping younger generations become more proficient at financial planning and money management.

Ed has an MBA degree in Finance and multiple professional certifications. His volunteering experience includes teaching basic money management skills to less-privileged students for Junior Achievement, and coaching youth athletic teams for baseball, softball, and soccer in Bergen County NJ. He is married with two children.

Making Big Money Decisions is Ed's second book. His first book, *Following Your Money*, was written in 2017 and is also available on Amazon. Ed founded DIYmoneytrack.com to share his unique personal money management perspective and methods for achieving financial independence and well-being.

Invest in Yourself!

If there are any questions or comments about the content being shared, please connect with Ed directly.

My contact information:

Website: **DIYmoneytrack.com**
Email: **ed@diymoneytrack.com**
LinkedIn: **www.linkedin.com/in/efdowns**

EXHIBITS

1. Major motives for rational and emotional spending
2. A rationalization process for making big and small money purchasing decisions
3. Impact of fund expenses on your returns (FINRA Fund Analyzer)
4. Example of how financing the purchase of a vehicle can reduce your resale value
5. Example of how to calculate the IOC from the difference in TCO
6. Other housing-related expenditures as a percent of household spending
7. Average annual incremental cost of adding from one to four children to a family
8. Average Costs Of Attendance (COA) by institution type

ENDNOTES

1   Buy Now, Pay Later (BNPL): What It Is, How It Works, Pros and Cons. Investopedia.com

2   The True Cost of Owning a Dog or Cat. Credit.com. July 2023.

3   How to plan for rising healthcare costs. Fidelity.com. Assumes couple aged 65 retiring in 2023.

4   Health Care Inflation in the United States (1948-2023). US Inflation Calculator. Average of annual inflation rates from 2018-2022.

5   The Cost of Caring for an Elderly Parent, Regions Bank (https://www.regions.com)

6   A brand is a product, service or concept that is publicly distinguished from other products, services or concepts so that it can be easily communicated and usually marketed. Source: TechTarget.

7   Baba Shiv: How to Make Better Decisions. Stanford Business School. YouTube: https://www.youtube.com/watch?v=SS4F1U5FuNM

8   69% of Americans Admit to Emotional Spending, Pushing 39% of Them Into Debt. Lendingtree.com. Sept 2023.

9   8 Psychological Traps in Home Buying and How to Avoid Them, Zillow.com

10 Global ad spending on track to top $1T for first time, WARC says. MarketingDive.com. Aug 2023.

11 Inflation is the rate of increase in prices over a given period of time.

12 Is Inflation High Compared to Years Past? Breaking Down Inflation Rates by Year. Forbes.com

13 College tuition inflation: How the cost of college has risen over time. Bankrate.com (July 2023)

14 How to keep your money from losing purchasing power. Bankrate.com

15 Assumes 25% tax rate.

16 12-month percentage change, Consumer Price Index, selected categories. US BLS: https://www.bls.gov/charts/consumer-price-index/consumer-price-index-by-category-line-chart.htm

17 How to maximize the money you make from payments. DIYmoneytrack.com

18 Chris Hogan, author of the book, Retired Inspired

19 How Do You Stack Up When It Comes to Retirement? Kiplinger.com. June 2023.

20 The average Social Security check increased this year due to inflation: Here's how much it is. CNBC.com. July 2023.

21 U.S. Bureau of Labor Statistics Consumer Expenditure Survey (Table 4500). 2022 data for 65 and older age range. Mean monthly expenditures range from $4,191 for renter to $4,566 for a dwelling owner.

22 What Is the Average Retirement Savings in the U.S.? The Motley Fool. Nov 2023.

23 Americans Facing a New Retirement Reality. Allianz Life Insurance Company of North America. May 2023.

24 Bankrate Retirement Calculator URL: https://www.bankrate.com/retirement/retirement-plan-calculator/

25 The actual savings rate may be lower depending on employer matching program and investment rate of return. Includes social security.

26 Assumes annual retirement expenses of $193,252, which is 80% of last year of income ($241,565).

27 No, Your Social Security Benefits Aren't Going Away. Feldman, Kiplinger.com.

28 How Long Will Your Savings Last? https://ffcalcs.com/how_long

29 What Does the S&P 500 Index Measure and How Is It Calculated? Investopedia.com (July 2023)

30 Mutual Fund vs. ETF: What's the Difference? Investopedia.com

31 Officialdata.org: https://www.officialdata.org/us/stocks/s-p-500/1993?amount=100&endYear=2023

32 Mutual Funds That Consistently Beat the Market? Not One of 2,132. NY Times. Dec 2022,

33 What Is a Good Expense Ratio for Mutual Funds? Investopedia.com (April 2021)

34 FINRA Fund Analyzer Resources: Annual Operating Expenses. Represents a fund's net operating expenses.

35 For illustrative purposes only. Analysis is not a recommendation to buy or sell these types of specific investments. Source: FINRA Fund Analyzer, Nov 2023.

36 Assumes investment held for 10 years, initial contribution of $10k, and 5% annual rate of return.

37 https://tools.finra.org/fund_analyzer/

38 According to KBB.com. Actual trade-in value offered by dealership could be higher or lower, but would most likely be lower. Seller could also sell car privately.

39 Leasing vs. Buying a New Car. Consumer Reports. Jon Linkov. Sept 2023.

40 Lease Vs. Buy A Car: https://www.bankrate.com/loans/auto-loans/lease-vs-buy-calculator/

41 Assumes 6.5% average annual rate of return.

42 Excludes financing costs, since those were already captured under calculation of funding IOC. 5-year TCO. Source: Edmunds.com.

43 Property Brothers Drew and Jonathan Scott break down the No. 1 thing you should do before house hunting. CNBC.com, Nov 2023.

44 When Renting Is Smarter Than Buying. Kiplinger.com

45 Rent vs. Buy Calculator: https://www.zillow.com/rent-vs-buy-calculator

46 Consumer Expenditure Survey. US Bureau of Labor Statistics. 2022

47 https://www.nerdwallet.com/mortgages/how-much-house-can-i-afford

48 Consumer Expenditure Survey. US Bureau of Labor Statistics. Consumer Income Before Taxes (2022 data).

49 Real Estate vs. Stocks: Which Has Higher Returns? U.S. News, Nov, 2023.

50 What is a reverse mortgage? Consumer Financial Protection Bureau: https://www.consumerfinance.gov/ask-cfpb/what-is-a-reverse-mortgage-en-224/

51 Mortgage Calculator. Bankrate.com.

52 Commentary: It's getting more expensive to raise children. And government isn't doing much to help. Brookings Institute. Aug 2022.

53 Family Budget Calculator. Economic Policy Institute. https://www.epi.org/resources/budget/

54 The Economic Policy Institute's Family Budget Calculator Technical Documentation. https://www.epi.org/publication/family-budget-calculator-documentation/

55   Average Cost of College & Tuition. Education Data Initiative (educationdata.org). Update Nov 2023.

56   Potential future financial value after 30-years of investing the cost of four years of public in-state ($104,108) or private college ($223,360) at 6.5% rate of return.

57   The College Payoff: More Education Doesn't Always Mean More Earnings. Georgetown University Center on Education and the Workforce.

58   The COA refers to the total cost of tuition and fees, books and supplies, as well as room and board for those students living on campus. COA does not include transportation costs, daily living expenses, student loan interest, etc. Source: Education Data Initiative

59   College Savings Calculator: Education cost inflation. Bankrate.com

60   Which US higher education institutions offer the best ROI? DIYmoneytrack.com. Highest CES – Avg Total Cost at All Family Income Levels.

61   Fun Money = Income minus necessary living expenses and pre-tax savings

62   DIYmoneytrack.com - Using playbook and tools: https://diymoneytrack.com/money-playbook/

63   $700k in retirement savings (401k's and Roth IRA's) and $150k in shorter duration savings and fixed income investments.

64   Bankrate.com Retirement Calculator: https://www.bankrate.com/retirement/retirement-plan-calculator/

65   What is private mortgage insurance? Consumer Financial Protection Bureau: https://www.consumerfinance.gov/ask-cfpb/what-is-private-mortgage-insurance-en-122

66   What Is a 529 Plan? Saving for College: https://www.savingforcollege.com/intro-to-529s/what-is-a-529-plan

www.ingramcontent.com/pod-product-compliance
Lightning Source LLC
Chambersburg PA
CBHW071618040426
42452CB00009B/1380